Consumer Guide for Reading Your Credit Report

BY

Wilfred Coombs

Consumer Guide for Reading Your Credit Report

First Printing, June 2013

Published by DebtPros21.

DebtPros21 is dedicated to educating consumers about the credit industry. For more information please visit our website at *www.debtpros21.com*, or write to us at:

DebtPros21
401 Cooper St.
Taylor, PA 18517

Author: Wilfred Coombs
Chief Editor: Kenn Anderson, Jr.
Layout and Design: Kenn Anderson, Jr.

ISBN13: 978-0-9895831-5-2

Foreword

As you are in the process of solving your debt issues, the most important first step is to get a copy of you tri-merged credit report and read through it **carefully**!! Make sure that all of the information on your report is correct and current. That includes only the information on the various credit lines, but your core information, such as name address and social security number as well. Over the years we have seen numerous credit reports that have combined credit histories of two or more persons because their core information has been erroneously mixed together mixed together.

Wilfred Coombs

Consumer Guide for Reading your Credit Report

Consumer Guide for Reading your Credit Report

YOUR CREDIT REPORT

To get a true and complete picture of your credit, you need to obtain a "tri-merge' credit report on yourself. A tri-merge report is a consolidated statement that combines information form all three of the major repositories. These are Experian, Equifax, and Trans Union. Your credit report is a summary of your credit profile at a given point in time. It provides you with an overview of all of your "trade lines." Trade lines are divided into four categories:

Open Accounts – Accounts that are active and also current. Payments are always made on time. In other words, accounts in good standing.

Closed Accounts – Accounts that are no longer active. They have been closed either by the consumer or by the creditor.

Derogatory Accounts – Active or closed accounts that have negative information. They can include the following:

a.) late payments

b.) accounts that have been charged off by the creditor.
c.) collection accounts – that have been referred to a collection agency for settlement.

Public Records – These can include liens or judgements that have been filed by a creditor to induce payment. It can also include a bankruptcy filing by the consumer.

HOW TO REVIEW YOUR TRADE LINES

Review each trade line carefully and verify all information. As you go down the list you can use the following as a guide for annotation.

1.) If the account does not belong to you, or contains outdated or incorrect information, place a **"?"** question mark in front of the creditor name.
2.) If the account has been paid, indicate by placing **PD** paid in front of the creditor name.
3.) If duplicate accounts are discovered, place the letter **D** in front of the creditor name for each duplicate.
4.) If the trade line information is accurate, indicate by placing **OK** in front of the creditor name.

DISPUTING ERRONEOUS INFORMATION

After you have reviewed all account information carefully, you must then begin to develop a strategy for correcting all of the errors you have identified. Your main goal is to correct the information with the respective credit repositories. There are a variety of ways you can accomplish this. The most basic method is to dispute by mail, however, all three of the major repositories now allow you to dispute on line. **Figure 1** is a sample letter you can use to dispute a trade line with the appropriate depository. As you can see, the letter must include complete information on each account, including:

- The Creditor Name
- The account number
- The address of the Creditor
- The reason for the dispute.

Repositories will accept only a limited list of reasons for disputes. These include the following:

- Not My Account
- Account Paid
- Duplicate Account
- Account is in Bankruptcy
- Account closed over 7 years.
- Judgment Satisfied
- Belongs to ex-spouse
- Corporate Account

Duplicate Accounts – An Analysis

Duplicate accounts are trade lines that appear on your credit report more than one time.

What Does Federal Law State Regarding Duplicate Accounts?

The Fair Credit Reporting Act, a federal law passed by congress to regulate the credit industry, states that an account cannot be listed more that once on a credit report. **But yet, it happens all the time!!** So why is it a problem for the consumer?? Because each trade line has a corresponding point deduction. In other words, you are losing points from your score at least twice for the same account!! For more information, see the Fair Credit Reporting Act at http://www.ftc.gov/os/statutes/031224fcra.pdf

HOW DO YOU IDENTIFY DUPLICATE ACCOUNTS ON YOUR REPORT?

The main incidents of duplicate accounts are when an account is delinquent and goes to collection. Once that occurs, the collections agency posts the account on your credit report. Unfortunately, there is no attempt to remove the trade line from the original creditor. As a result, the trade line now appears on your report twice under different account names.

You can recognize duplicate accounts by reading across the account line and identifying key information as being exactly the same or very similar. Key information fields include the following:

1.) **The Creditor Name** – On "open" accounts, both lines will have the same creditor name. This does not in itself, however, mean it's a duplicate.
2.) **The Account Number** – The account number will be the same or similar, meaning that only the last one or two digits are different.
3.) **The Credit Limit** – This field can be a key indicator of duplication. It represents your credit limit on a revolving account or your total obligation on a non revolving account. If these numbers are the same or very similar, it is probably not a coincidence.
4.) **The Current Balance** – If these numbers are exactly the same it is probably a duplicate account. If it is now the same but very close, the second account may be a duplicate with some carrying charges added.
5.) **The Date of Last Activity** – The last date of a reportable activity on an account is listed here. If these dates are the same *and one or more of the above criteria also matches*, it is another indicator of duplication.

IDENTIFYING DUPLICATION IN COLLECTION ACCOUNTS

When a creditor refers an account to collections status, there are a variety of approaches they may take in their attempt to collect the money they are owed. Some examples are:

1.) They can contract with a collection agency and offer them a commission if they collect the amount owed.
2.) They can sell the account to a collection agency, or to another lending agency, for an amount below that which is owed, leaving the new owner of the account to settle with the debtor.
3.) In many cases, they will contract with more that one collection agency on a commission basis at the same time, hoping to increase their chances of collecting.

COMMON WEAL	4540	4540	2	02/00	0	0	0	HL	23	0	22
NCO FINANC	4540	4540	22	04/03	0	0	0	Mon-Rev HL	28	26	28

To identify a duplicate collection account, you can use the same criteria as mentioned above for open ACCOUNTS, **except the creditor name will be different**. In the illustration above, you can see by the amounts owed that these are duplicates. The account has been registered once by the creditor (Commonwealth) and once by the collection agency (NCO) that has either been contracted to try and collect or now actually owns the account. Both the credit limit and the amount owed (4540) are exactly the same. These numbers are you key indicators that the account is a duplicate.

Do the Same Rules Apply?

Yes, the Fair Credit Reporting Act does not allow duplicate account information on a credit report. The fact that the creditor name is different for the collection agency than for the original creditor makes no difference. It is still considered a duplicate.

How to Proceed

If these types of duplicate accounts appear on your report, it will take time and effort on your part to have the problem corrected. Here are the steps you must take:

1.) You should be prepared to settle the account. Raise the money to pay the account in full. This will give you leverage.
2.) If it is a collection account, contact the original creditor and ask them if the account if it is still on file in their billing system. If they can access it, they still own it. If the creditor no longer owns the account, you will have to contact the collection agencies to determine who the new owner is.
3.) Inform the current creditor that you are ready to pay the account, but first they must agree to take certain actions.
    a.) Update you credit report
    b.) Send you a letter stating that the account has been paid in full and send a copy to the other collection agencies that are on the report as being associated to the account.
4.) As soon as you have received the letter, attach it to a dispute letter to the repositories and ask them to remove all trade lines from your report that are associated with this account. (See sample letter in **Figure 2**).

Disputing Online

It can take up to thirty days from the time you submit your letter to receive a response. Each repository is required, by law, to mail you a written response to your dispute within thirty days letting you know whether they agree with your requests. Even if they don't agree, all is not lost. Included in the response will be a file number or access code to enter you account on their website. All three websites contain instructions on how to dispute on line.

Finally, you can review your credit report and dispute errors free of charge by using a web site titled annualcreditreport.com. Please be advised that the repositories will only allow you use this site once year per repository at no cost to you.

Paying to Dispute

If you are on a tight time frame and need some quick action, you can contract the repositories or with other credit resellers to provide you with 24 to 48 hour service. This option can be expensive, however, so you should only use it if you have some urgency. Further on, you will find a list of websites of all the repositories as well as some credit resellers that offer the "paid" dispute service.

Your Credit Profile

A good credit score is directly related to a good credit profile. If you think of your credit report as a balance between the good and the bad, if your good stuff is not so good then just working on the bad or erroneous will not be sufficient to give you the score you want

The minimum requirements for a good credit score are as follows:

1.) You must have a minimum of three open accounts.
2.) Ideally, those accounts should include at least one mortgage and two credit cards.
3.) The three open accounts must appear in the record for all three repositories to have consistent scores across the board.

Obviously, there are some variations of this, but you should test these rules of thumb against your current report. If you do not meet this basic profile, there are a few things you can do:

1.) **Open new accounts** – the quickest way to increase your credit score is to open new revolving accounts, such as credit cards, or charge cards for a department store. If you are turned down due to a low score, try applying for a secured credit card. A web site that lists companies that offer secured cards is on page 15.
2.) **Charge something immediately** – As soon as you receive the card, charge something to it right way. It doesn't have to be anything big. A small amount will do.
3.) **Pay it off right way** – As soon as you receive the bill from the credit card company, send them a check the same day. Don't wait until the due date!! You need to be sure of a positive payment history on the account. Once you have completed the transaction, you can set the card aside and not use it again. It has served its purpose.

DEROGATORY ACCOUNTS

Once you have completed all of the steps previously mentioned, you r next task is to begin to resolve your problems with your derogatory accounts. The most effective method for attacking these problems is as follows:

1.) Go to list of derogatory accounts on your final analysis and mark any account you are in the process of disputing. If your disputes are legitimate, you can skip these and assume they are already in the process of being resolved. (see user guide for illustration).
2.) Review carefully each of the remaining accounts to determine whether they should be paid. Since your financial resources are limited, you should prioritize which accounts will give you the biggest "bang for your buck".
3.) Pay all of the accounts you can afford to pay down to zero. Re-

member to contact the creditor first and ask for an agreement for payment as described in **Figure 3.** A rule of thumb is you will gain back approximately half the point deductions you are currently losing for each account you pay down to zero. That assumes, however, that your overall credit profile meets the basic requirements as stipulated on page 4.

4.) Finally, don't expect to see the results of these payments immediately. It usually takes from 30 to 45 days for the updated information to be reflected on your report. **If you must also establish credit by taking on new accounts, you should work on both these problems simultaneously.** Everything should then come together within the six week time frame and your score will increase significantly.

PAYING OFF YOUR DEROGATORY ACCOUNTS

Once you have reached an agreement with the creditor, pay the balance by sending a certified check or money order. Do not use a personal check for the following reasons:

1.) Personal checks can take a long time to clear.
2.) Certified checks or money orders give you an instant receipt for the payment.
3.) If the creditor does not fulfill their part of the agreement, you can use the letter and the receipt as documentation to file a dispute directly with the repositories.

Creditor	AcctNo	HC	Bal	Mo	DLA	30	60	90	Status	XP	TU	EF
ALLIAN CE M	14000000 23153	47955	40596	107	12/02	3	0	4	1-30 HL	47	53	77
WACHO VIA B	10100024 32364	1008	1008	13	11/02	0	0	0	HL	40	45	0
CREDIT ECH	1714862	334	334	9	04/02	0	0	0	HL	40	45	0
NCO FINSY	10905035 44101207	18659	186 59	8 55	05/02 11/02				HL HL	0 0	0 45	65 65
COLLSP EC I	1343093	58	58	4	10/01				HL	0	45	0

In the example above, the Wachovia account has already been disputed. The Alliance account has late payments and a high balance. Paying this account down would not be an effective strategy at this time. We should focus on paying the bottom three accounts that have much lower balances and will allow us to gain a significant number of points once they are updated to a zero balance.

Applying for a Loan

There is an old saying in the business world. When you are going for a job interview, shine your shoes, when you are applying for a bank loan shine your balance sheet. Your balance sheet is your credit report. Before apply for a mortgage, start preparing at least a month in advance.

Here are some tips:

1.) Pay your credit card balances down as much as possible and don't incur any new debt during the month before you apply
2.) Schedule your appointment with the bank toward the end of the month to insure that all payments you made have been submitted to the credit repositories.
3.) Review your credit report carefully and make sure there are no errors.

Follow these simple rules and you can have peace of mind about your credit score!!

Rules of Thumb on Raising Credit Scores

A credit report is like a balance sheet. It is reflects a credit profile at a point in time. It contains both a positive side and a negative side. In order to significantly improve a credit score, both sides must be dealt with equally.

The Ideal Credit Profile

The ideal credit profile is at least five open accounts with each repository. An exact profile of these accounts is as follows:

- One current mortgage
- One current car loan
- Three current credit cards

Open Accounts

When you begin to review your credit report, first look at the number of open accounts. If the number is zero or less than 3, this problem must be addressed first. Open more accounts, preferably credit cards. If the customer's score is too low for them to obtain a "normal" card, they can usually get a secured card through creditcards.com or credit-infocenter.com.

As soon as you receive the card, you should charge a small amount to it. As little as twenty dollars is sufficient. As soon as they receive their statement, they should pay the balance immediately and not wait for the due date. Once these transactions have been completed, the customer can set the secured card aside and not use it and not use it again for another month.

Disputing

Successfully removing a trade line from a credit report through the dispute process is the most effective means of raising a credit score. For example, the customer finds a trade line on their credit report which does not belong to them. A dispute letter is then sent to the appropriate repositories requesting the account be removed. If the repositories agree and remove the account, one hundred percent of the point deductions associated with that account will be eliminated.

Paying Down Balances on Revolving Acounts

The current balance is not necessarily a relevant factor in deciding which revolving accounts to pay down. The reason is that the ratio of the balance to the high credit limit is the determining factor in how many points you are losing on your score.

For example, an account that has a current balance of fifty percent of the credit limit will cost you many more points than on that has a twenty five percent balance.

The most important thing you must keep in mind as you are prioritizing your accounts for payment is the goal is to reach a ratio that is below twenty five percent of the high credit. You can do this by paying down the balance, raising the credit limit, or both.
This principle applies in all revolving accounts, whether they are "open" or "derogatory".

DISPUTING CLOSED ACCOUNTS

A third tactic you can use to reduce points it to dispute closed accounts whose date of last activity is more that seven (7) years and request removal. Even though the point deductions for each tradeline line is small. If the total number of trade lines is above twenty, it can make a difference.

REQUESTING REMOVAL OF PAID ACCOUNTS

The Fair Credit Reporting Act states that derogatory trade line can remain in your credit report for **up to** seven years. This is a maximum not a minimum. Your creditor can remove the tradeline form your report at any time. That gives you the option of requesting its removal as part of your settlement agreement with them.

As an example, let's assume you find an unpaid medical bill on your credit report that you expected your medical insurance would cover. The tradeline has been added to you report by a collection agency and is a relatively small amount, such as an x-ray, that you can settle immediately. You contact the agency and offer to settle the account in full if they also agree to remove the tradeline form your credit report as soon as payment is received. There is no good reason for them to deny this request. Therefore, you should be somewhat insistent that they agree.

Credit Bureau name
Street Address or P.O. Box
City, State, Zip

Attn: Customer Service

I recently had the opportunity to review my credit report and I discovered some erroneous information being reported by your company. A summary of this information is as follows:

Creditor Name	Creditor Address	Account Number	Description of Error

These errors are having a negative effect on my credit rating and I would appreciate if you could correct them as soon as possible, since I am in the process of applying for a mortgage.

Your prompt attention to this matter will be greatly appreciated.

Sincerely,

Attachments: Ex: Documentation of payment if account is closed.

Figure 1 - Sample Dispute Letter (Repositories)

Credit Bureau name
Street Address or P.O. Box
City, State, Zip

Attn: Customer Service

I recently had the opportunity to review my credit report and I discovered some erroneous information being reported by your company. A summary of this information is as follows:

Creditor Name	Creditor Address	Account Number	Description of Error

As you can see, these are the same account reported by two different entities. Attached you will find letter from the original/ current creditor, stipulating that the account has been paid in full. Accordingly, I hereby request that you update my report and remove all trade lines including those of the original/current creditor.

These errors are having a negative effect on my credit rating and I would appreciate if you could correct them as soon as possible, since I am in the process of applying for a mortgage.

Your prompt attention to this matter will be greatly appreciated.

Sincerely,

Figure 2 - Sample Dispute Letter (Duplicate Accounts)

Company Name
Contact person
Street Address
City/State/Zip

RE: Account Settlement
(Member Name)
SS# ACCT#

Dear

I am currently in the process of improving my credit and settling my derogatory accounts. I am both willing and able to settle the above account immediately. Specifically, I am ready to do the following:

Make payment in the amount of (state terms and amounts)

In return I request that your company take the following actions to correct the credit report:

Update my credit information to the appropriate entities.

If you agree to the above, please indicate by signing at the bottom of this document and return faxing to me at the number listed above. I will then make payment arrangements as soon as possible. In addition, please prepare to submit the necessary reporting forms to the following credit bureaus.

(List names of all repositories reporting)

Under the provisions of Section 168 of the Fair Credit Reporting Act, I am entitled to notification that these items have been deleted. Accordingly, I would appreciate if you would send me a copy of your request to each credit bureau at the address listed above.

Thank you in advance for your cooperation.

Sincerely,

We Agree________________________________

(Please Indicate Name and Title)

Figure 3 - Sample Dispute Letter (Creditors)

Federal Trade Commission
March 1999

Your credit report—a type of consumer report—contains information about where you work and live and how you pay your bills. It also may show whether you've been sued or arrested or have filed for bankruptcy. Companies called consumer reporting agencies (CRAs) or credit bureaus compile and sell your credit report to businesses. Because businesses use this information to evaluate your applications for credit, insurance, employment, and other purposes allowed by the Fair Credit Reporting Act (FCRA), it's important that the information in your report is complete and accurate.

Some financial advisors suggest that you periodically review your credit report for inaccuracies or omissions. This could be especially important if you're considering making a major purchase, such as buying a home. Checking in advance on the accuracy of information in your credit file could speed the credit-granting process.

Getting Your Credit Report

If you've been denied credit, insurance, or employment because of information supplied by a CRA, the FCRA says the company you applied to must give you the CRA's name, address, and telephone number. If you contact the agency for a copy of your report within 60 days of receiving a denial notice, the report is free. In addition, you're entitled to one free copy of your report a year if you can prove that (1) you're unemployed and plan to look for a job within 60 days, (2) you're on welfare, or (3) your report is inaccurate because of fraud. Otherwise, a CRA may charge you up to $9.00 for a copy of your report.

If you simply want a copy of your report, call the CRAs listed in the Yellow Pages under "credit" or "credit rating and reporting." Call each credit bureau listed since more than one agency may have a file on you, some with different information. The three major national credit bureaus are:

Equifax
P.O. Box 740241
Atlanta, GA 30374-0241
(800) 685-1111

Experian
P.O. Box 2002
Allen, TX 75013
(888) EXPERIAN
(888-397-3742)

Trans Union
P.O. Box 1000
Chester, PA 19022
(800) 916-8800

Correcting Errors

Under the FCRA, both the CRA and the organization that provided the information to the CRA, such as a bank or credit card company, have responsibilities for correcting inaccurate or incomplete information in your report. To protect all your rights under the law, contact both the CRA and the information provider.

First, tell the CRA in writing what information you believe is inaccurate. Include copies (NOT originals) of documents that support your position. In addition to providing your complete name and address, your letter should clearly identify each item in your report you dispute, state the facts and explain why you dispute the information, and request deletion or correction. You may want to enclose a copy of your report with the items in question circled. Your letter may look something like the sample. Send your letter by certified mail, return receipt requested, so you can document what the CRA received. Keep copies of your dispute letter and enclosures.

CRAs must reinvestigate the items in question—usually within 30 days—unless they consider your dispute frivolous. They also must forward all relevant data you provide about the dispute to the information provider. After the information provider receives notice of a dispute from the CRA, it must investigate, review all relevant information provided by the CRA, and report the results to the CRA. If the information provider finds the disputed information to be inaccurate, it must notify all nationwide CRAs so they can correct this information in your file.

Disputed information that cannot be verified must be deleted from your file. If your report contains erroneous information, the CRA must correct it. If an item is incomplete, the CRA must complete it. For example, if your file showed that you were late making payments, but failed to show that you were no longer delinquent, the CRA must show that you're current. If your file shows an account that belongs only to another person, the CRA must delete it.

When the reinvestigation is complete, the CRA must give you the written results and a free copy of your report if the dispute results in a change. If an item is changed or removed, the CRA cannot put the disputed information back in your file unless the information provider verifies its accuracy and completeness, and the CRA gives you a written notice that includes the name, address, and phone number of the provider.

Also, if you request, the CRA must send notices of corrections to anyone who received your report in the past six months. Job applicants can have a corrected copy of their report sent to anyone who received a copy during the past two years for employment purposes. If a reinvestigation does not resolve your dispute, ask the CRA to include your statement of the dispute in your file and in future reports.

Second, in addition to writing to the CRA, tell the creditor or other information provider in writing that you dispute an item. Again, include copies (NOT originals) of documents that support your position. Many providers specify an address for disputes. If the provider then reports the item to any CRA, it must include a notice of your dispute. In addition, if you are correct—that is, if the disputed information is not accurate—the information provider may not use it again.

ACCURATE NEGATIVE INFORMATION

When negative information in your report is accurate, only the passage of time can assure its removal. Accurate negative information can generally stay on your report for 7 years. There are certain exceptions: Information about criminal convictions may be reported without any time limitation. Bankruptcy information may be reported for 10 years. Credit information reported in response to an application for a job with a salary of more than $75,000 has no time limit.

Credit information reported because of an application for more than $150,000 worth of credit or life insurance has no time limit. Information about a lawsuit or an unpaid judgment against you can be reported for seven years or until the statute of limitations runs out, whichever is longer.

ADDING ACCOUNTS TO YOUR FILE

Your credit file may not reflect all your credit accounts. Although most national department store and all-purpose bank credit card accounts will be included in your file, not all creditors supply information to CRAs: Some travel, entertainment, gasoline card companies, local retailers, and credit unions are among those creditors that don't.

If you've been told you were denied credit because of an "insufficient credit file" or "no credit file" and you have accounts with creditors that don't appear in your credit file, ask the CRA to add this information to future reports. Although they are not required to do so, many CRAs will add verifiable accounts for a fee. You should, however, understand that if these creditors do not report to the CRA on a regular basis, these added items will not be updated in your file.

FOR MORE INFORMATION

The FTC works for the consumer to prevent fraudulent, deceptive and unfair business practices in the marketplace and to provide information to help consumers spot, stop and avoid them. To file a complaint or to get free information on consumer issues, visit www.ftc.gov or call toll-free, 1-877-FTC-HELP (1-877-382-4357); TTY: 1-866-653-4261. The FTC enters Internet, telemarketing, identity theft and other fraud-related complaints into Consumer Sentinel, a secure, online database available to hundreds of civil and criminal law enforcement agencies in the U

LIST OF WEB SITES THAT OFFER ONLINE DISPUTING

- Aircredit.com (for subscribers only)
- Creditplus.com (for subscribers only)
- Clearcredit.com
- Experian.com
- Equifax.com
- Transunion.com

BUYER BEWARE!! Please be aware that are not recommending any of these companies. We are providing this information for your convenience only.

SECURED CREDIT CARDS

There are a number of credit card companies that will offer you a card. Go to their respective web sites and read their terms carefully. In most cases their interest rates will be high but you will not have to worry about the rate if you follow the procedures described earlier. For more information on who offers these cards, go to the web site below.

http://www.creditcard321.com/secured-credit-cards?lp=1

TIPS ON KEEPING YOUR CREDIT SCORE HIGH

Here are some ways you can help yourself to maintain a good score:

1.) Pay your bills on time. Late payments can be a serious impediment to improving your score. Recent late payments carry the most serious deductions.
2.) Do not incur new debt. If you already have sufficient open accounts, do not incur any new debt. Additional accounts with so payment history can lower your score. If you need to acquire new accounts to improve your credit score, remember that they may lower you score initially, but once you begin making payments you score will improve.
3.) Be careful about shopping for credit.. If you apply to any financial or consumer credit company, such as a car dealer, insurance company, bank or mortgage company without contacting us first. They will "pull" your credit report and it will cost you points on your score. If necessary, pay to have your credit report pulled yourself. Each of the three major repositories now offer this service and it won't count against your score.
4.) Keep credit balances low. You credit card balances should never exceed twenty (25) five percent of your high credit limit. If you cannot meet this requirement, apply for a higher limit to lower your ratio.
5.) Avoid Collection Status – Never let you bills lapse to this point. Once the creditor refers your account to a collection agency, it will automatically be placed on your credit report as a collections account.

For more information, please check out these other publications from DebtPros21.

Reading Your Credit Report

This book guides you through each individual trade line and tells you the significance of each piece of information as it applies to your credit worthiness, as well as the proper procedures for disputing errors on your credit information.

The Credit Industry - A Primer

Learn about how to read your credit report, protect yourself from predatory lenders and debt collectors, as well as how to safeguard yourself from credit fraud and identity theft.

The Ten Commandments of Credit

Intended to be used after your credit has been restored, *The Ten Commandments of Credit* will give you the information you need in order to maintain excellent credit worthiness.

ISBN 978-0-9895831-5-2
9 780989 583152

Made in the USA
Monee, IL
04 November 2026

67387015R00017